TEAM SPIRIT®

SMART BOOKS FOR YOUNG FANS

30 ► 20 ► 10 ►

THE KANSAS CITY CHIEFS

BY
MARK STEWART

New Hanover County Public Library
201 Chestnut Street
Wilmington, North Carolina 28401

NORWOOD HOUSE PRESS

CHICAGO, ILLINOIS

Norwood House Press
P.O. Box 316598
Chicago, Illinois 60631

For information regarding Norwood House Press, please visit our website at:
www.norwoodhousepress.com or call 866-565-2900.

All photos courtesy of Getty Images except the following:
Black Book Partners (8, 9, 10, 11, 14, 22, 25, 30, 35 top right & bottom, 37, 38, 39, 40, 42 bottom, 43 bottom, 45),
Topps, Inc. (15, 16, 18, 20, 21, 23, 27, 28, 31, 34 both, 41, 42 top & bottom left, 43 top),
Author's Collection (33), Kansas City Chiefs/NFL (35 top left, 36 bottom), Matt Richman (48).
Cover Photo: Icon SMI

The memorabilia and artifacts pictured in this book are presented for educational and informational purposes,
and come from the collection of the author.

Editor: Mike Kennedy
Designer: Ron Jaffe
Project Management: Black Book Partners, LLC.
Special thanks to Topps, Inc.

Library of Congress Cataloging-in-Publication Data

Stewart, Mark, 1960-
   The Kansas City Chiefs / by Mark Stewart.
      p. cm. -- (Team spirit)
   Includes bibliographical references and index.
   Summary: "A revised Team Spirit Football edition featuring the Kansas City
Chiefs that chronicles the history and accomplishments of the team. Includes
access to the Team Spirit website which provides additional information and
photos"--Provided by publisher.
   ISBN 978-1-59953-527-2 (library edition : alk. paper) -- ISBN
978-1-60357-469-3 (ebook)
   1. Kansas City Chiefs (Football team)--History--Juvenile literature. I.
Title.
   GV956.K35S84 2012
   796.332'6409778411--dc23
                                        2012014904

Manufactured in the United States of America in North Mankato, Minnesota.
205N—082012

COVER PHOTO: The Chiefs celebrate a touchdown with their fans.

Table of Contents

ABOUT OUR GLOSSARY

In this book, there may be several words that you are reading for the first time. Some are sports words, some are new vocabulary words, and some are familiar words that are used in an unusual way. All of these words are defined on page 46. Throughout the book, sports words appear in **bold type**. Regular vocabulary words appear in ***bold italic type***.

Meet the Chiefs

When a team has been around for more than 50 years, its fans don't expect many surprises. The Kansas City Chiefs are the exception to that rule. They put their team together like a jigsaw puzzle, fitting different players with different talents into an exciting "big picture."

Throughout their history, the Chiefs have won in a variety of ways. Sometimes, they depend on speed to give them an advantage. Other times, they overpower their opponents. Smart decisions also are a *trademark* of Kansas City football.

This book tells the story of the Chiefs. Each year, they look at their strengths and build their team around the skills of a few breathtaking stars. The Chiefs are never afraid to try something new. Needless to say, fans in Kansas City have come to love surprises … and to expect the unexpected.

Derrick Johnson and his Kansas City teammates give head coach Romeo Crennel a victory shower.

Glory Days

Lamar Hunt was a man who was used to getting his way. He made millions in the energy business and was one of the most recognizable people in Texas. One thing *eluded* Hunt: a team in the **National Football League (NFL)**. His solution was to start a league of his own, the **American Football League (AFL)**. The AFL played its first season in 1960. The name of Hunt's team was the Dallas Texans.

The NFL fought back by putting its own team in Dallas. The Cowboys also played their first season in 1960. Hunt had a trick up his sleeve. He hired Hank Stram to coach the Texans. Stram was a young coach who loved to try new ideas. He also knew how to find talented players. Among the Dallas stars in the early 1960s were quarterback Cotton Davidson, linemen Jerry Mays and E.J. Holub, and linebacker Sherrill Headrick.

The team's best player was running back Abner Haynes. He was named **Rookie** of the Year and Player of the Year in his first season. Haynes led the AFL in rushing touchdowns in each of his first three seasons.

In 1962, the Texans signed quarterback Len Dawson. He led Dallas to its first AFL championship that same season. Other stars on that team included Jim Tyrer, Fred Arbanas, Chris Burford, Bobby Hunt, and Johnny Robinson. A few months after their victory, the Texans moved to Kansas City, Missouri, and became the Chiefs. Hunt no longer wanted to compete with the Cowboys, and Kansas City fans were hungry for a team.

The AFL and NFL joined forces in 1970. During the AFL's 10 years, the Chiefs had the league's best record at 87 wins, 48 losses, and five ties. They won three championships in all. The Chiefs played in the first **Super Bowl** in 1967 and lost to the Green Bay Packers. They returned to the big game three years later and beat the Minnesota Vikings.

LEFT: Lamar Hunt
ABOVE: Len Dawson calls a play in the Kansas City huddle.

Kansas City had a well-balanced team during the 1960s. Running back Mike Garrett and receiver Otis Taylor starred with Dawson on offense. The defense was led by Buck Buchanan, Bobby Bell, Willie Lanier, and Emmitt Thomas. Jan Stenerud was the team's kicker.

Once they joined the NFL, the Chiefs played in the competitive **Western Division** of the **American Football Conference (AFC)**. During the 1970s and 1980s, they struggled to finish ahead of the Oakland Raiders, Denver Broncos, and San Diego Chargers. Kansas City fans still had some exciting players to root for, including receivers Stephon Paige and Carlos Carlson, quarterbacks Bill Kenney and Steve DeBerg, running back Christian Okoye, and defensive stars Art Still, Deron Cherry, and Albert Lewis.

In the early 1990s, the Chiefs returned to their winning ways. They were led by two NFL legends, Joe Montana and Marcus Allen. Young pass-rushers Derrick Thomas and Neil Smith turned

LEFT: Derrick Thomas zeroes in on the quarterback.
ABOVE: Marcus Allen catches his breath between plays.

Kansas City's defense into one of the toughest in the league. In 1993, the Chiefs made it all the way to the **AFC Championship Game**. Smith and Thomas carried the team to two more **AFC West** titles, but a third trip to the Super Bowl was just beyond their grasp.

The Chiefs began the 21st century with high hopes and great expectations. Their fans dreamed of another Super Bowl victory. Kansas City searched for the right combination of players to make that happen. They found some of the game's most exciting young stars and fought hard to take control of the AFC West away from the Raiders, Chargers, and Broncos. This was not an easy task.

The Chiefs looked to their past in order to plan their future. They built their offense around quarterbacks Trent Green and Matt Cassel. They put the ball in the hands of talented runners

Priest Holmes, Larry Johnson, and Jamaal Charles. They found sure-handed receivers in Derrick Alexander and Dwayne Bowe. And the defense starred dynamic players such as linebackers Derrick Johnson and Tamba Hali.

The team's greatest player during this time was tight end Tony Gonzalez. He was big enough to play *professional* basketball and quick enough to be a receiver. In 12 years in Kansas City, Gonzalez was named **All-Pro** five times.

To the great delight of Kansas City fans, the Chiefs improved at the same time as the other teams in the AFC West were struggling. Their timing couldn't have been better. The Chiefs reached the **playoffs** in 2010 and began building a new winning *tradition* to carry them to their next championship.

LEFT: Neil Smith
ABOVE: Tony Gonzalez

Home Turf

Before they moved to Kansas City, the Chiefs played in Dallas as the Texans. Their home field, the Cotton Bowl, was one of the most famous stadiums in football. The Chiefs' first home in Kansas City was Municipal Stadium. They shared it with the Kansas City Athletics baseball team and later with the Kansas City Royals baseball team.

Lamar Hunt always wanted a stadium of his own. He got it in 1972, when the Chiefs moved to Arrowhead Stadium. They played on *artificial turf* until 1994, when the team changed to a natural grass field. The stadium went through major changes starting in 2007. Among the improvements were the addition of the Chiefs Hall of Honor and an area that pays tribute to Hunt.

BY THE NUMBERS

- The Chiefs' stadium has 76,416 seats.
- It is the fourth-largest NFL stadium in the United States.
- The cost to renovate the stadium was $375 million.

Arrowhead Stadium is a sea of red for a game between the Chiefs and the Cincinnati Bengals.

Dressed for Success

Kansas City's colors are red, gold, and white. The team's uniform is one of the best-looking in the NFL. The Texans wore similar uniforms when they played in Dallas. Lamar Hunt liked them and kept the same colors when the team became the Chiefs.

The Chiefs have used the same helmet design since 1963. It shows a white arrowhead on a red background, with the letters *KC* written in red. Like the team's uniform, the Kansas City helmet is a **classic**.

Most fans believe that the name "Chiefs" was inspired by Native-American leaders. But the name actually came from the mayor of Kansas City during the 1960s. H. Roe Bartle

FRED ARBANAS **end**

made the team a generous offer to move from Dallas in 1963, and Hunt chose the new name as a *thank you*. Bartle was a leader of the Boy Scouts of America, and everyone called him the "Chief."

LEFT: Dwayne Bowe's uniform is almost identical to the one used by the Chiefs in the 1960s.   **ABOVE**: Fred Arbanas poses for this 1960s card in the team's home jersey.

We Won!

In 1962, the Dallas Texans won the AFL championship. After the team moved to Kansas City, the Chiefs claimed two more AFL titles. They also made it to the Super Bowl twice and won the big game once.

In their first championship season, the Texans were led by Len Dawson, Jim Tyrer, Fred Arbanas, and Johnny Robinson. These four

ABNER HAYNES
HALFBACK
DALLAS TEXANS

stars played for the team in each if its three AFL championships. In their first AFL title game, the Texans faced the Houston Oilers. Abner Haynes scored two touchdowns in the first half to help Dallas to a 17–0 lead. The Oilers fought back in the second half and tied the game with five minutes left in the fourth quarter.

The contest went into **overtime**. Neither team scored in the first 15-minute period. Tommy Brooker gave the Texans

their first championship when he connected on a **field goal** in the second overtime period. His kick ended the longest game in pro football history.

Four years later, the team won its first AFL crown as the Chiefs. This time, they played the Buffalo Bills in the 1966 championship game. The winner would face the NFL champions in the first Super Bowl. The Chiefs had added more great players, including receiver Otis Taylor, running back Mike Garrett, and defensive stars Buck Buchanan, Bobby Bell, Jerry Mays, Emmitt Thomas, and Fred Williamson.

In the **AFL Championship Game**, the Bills had no chance. Dawson hit Arbanas and Taylor for touchdowns, and Garrett scored

LEFT: Abner Haynes   **ABOVE**: Mike Garrett takes a handoff from Len Dawson in the 1966 AFL title game.

EMMITT
THOMAS

CORNERBACK
CHIEFS

twice on runs. Buffalo could do nothing when it had the ball, and the Chiefs won 31–7. Two weeks later, Kansas City played the Green Bay Packers in Super Bowl I. The Chiefs lost 35–10.

The Chiefs were determined to get back to the Super Bowl and win it. In 1969, they defeated the New York Jets in the playoffs, and then faced their greatest *rivals*, the Oakland Raiders, in the last AFL Championship Game. The Chiefs had lost twice to Oakland in the regular season, but they came out on top this time. Their pass rush was unstoppable, and Thomas **intercepted** two passes. Kansas City won 17–7.

The Chiefs met the Minnesota Vikings in Super Bowl IV. Kansas City was the more experienced team, but the Vikings had loads of talent. Their defense was nicknamed the "Purple People Eaters." They also had a terrific running attack. The Chiefs knew what it took to win a championship and quickly got down to business.

Kansas City controlled the pace of the game. The Chiefs gobbled up yards on the ground and kept Dawson safe in the pocket. He

had all the time he needed to find open receivers. Jan Stenerud kicked three field goals, and the Chiefs scored two touchdowns to win 23–7. In Kansas City's 10th season, the team stood atop the pro football world.

LEFT: Emmitt Thomas
ABOVE: Hank Stram gets a victory ride after Super Bowl IV.

Go-To Guys

To be a true star in the NFL, you need more than fast feet and a big body. You have to be a "go-to guy"—someone the coach wants on the field at the end of a big game. Chiefs fans have had a lot to cheer about over the years, including these great stars ...

THE PIONEERS

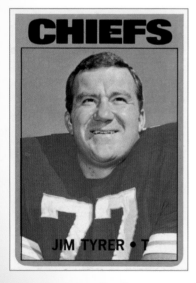

CHIEFS

JIM TYRER • T

JIM TYRER   Offensive Lineman

- BORN: 2/25/1939   • DIED: 9/15/1980
- PLAYED FOR TEAM: 1961 TO 1973

Jim Tyrer led one of football's best offensive lines in the 1960s and early 1970s. He was a great blocker who towered over his opponents. Tyrer was named **All-AFL** eight years in a row.

LEN DAWSON   Quarterback

- BORN: 6/20/1935   • PLAYED FOR TEAM: 1962 TO 1975

Len Dawson played with great *poise*. He rarely made a bad pass and never panicked when the Chiefs were trailing. Dawson was the **Most Valuable Player (MVP)** of Super Bowl IV and entered the **Hall of Fame** in 1987.

BOBBY BELL   Linebacker

- BORN: 6/17/1940   • PLAYED FOR TEAM: 1963 TO 1974

Bobby Bell was an amazing athlete who could have played anywhere on the field. He used his quick hands and feet to chase down running backs and **sack** the quarterback. Bell was named All-AFL as a defensive end in 1964 and All-AFL as a linebacker in 1965.

BUCK BUCHANAN   Defensive Lineman

- BORN: 9/10/1940   • PLAYED FOR TEAM: 1963 TO 1975

Buck Buchanan was the top pick in the 1963 AFL draft. He was fast enough to tackle runners along the sidelines and tall enough to knock down passes that others could not reach. Buchanan was voted All-Pro four times.

BUCK BUCHANAN
KANSAS CITY CHIEFS
DEFENSIVE TACKLE

EMMITT THOMAS   Defensive Back

- BORN: 6/3/1943   • PLAYED FOR TEAM: 1966 TO 1978

Emmitt Thomas had a knack for knowing where an opponent's next pass was headed. He led the league in interceptions twice. After he retired, Thomas returned to Kansas City to join the team's coaching staff.

WILLIE LANIER   Linebacker

- BORN: 8/21/1945   • PLAYED FOR TEAM: 1967 TO 1977

Willie Lanier was a hard tackler and good pass defender. He was the first African American to star at middle linebacker. Many believed that Lanier was the best player at his position during the 1970s.

LEFT: Jim Tyrer
ABOVE: Buck Buchanan

DERON CHERRY   Defensive Back

- BORN: 9/12/1959   • PLAYED FOR TEAM: 1981 TO 1991

Deron Cherry was one of the NFL's best players in the 1980s. He made the **Pro Bowl** six times and finished his career with 50 interceptions. After he retired, he became an owner of the Jacksonville Jaguars.

NEIL SMITH   Defensive Lineman

- BORN: 4/10/1966   • PLAYED FOR TEAM: 1988 TO 1996

Neil Smith played defensive end opposite Derrick Thomas. This gave the Chiefs All-Pro pass-rushers on both sides of the field. Smith led the NFL in sacks in 1993. He made the Pro Bowl six times.

DERRICK THOMAS   Linebacker

- BORN: 1/1/1967   • DIED: 2/8/2000   • PLAYED FOR TEAM: 1989 TO 1999

Derrick Thomas terrified quarterbacks. He was too big and fast for one player to block him, and opponents never knew when or where he would burst across the line. In his second season, Thomas led the NFL with 20 sacks.

WILL SHIELDS   Offensive Lineman

- BORN: 9/15/1971   • PLAYED FOR TEAM: 1993 TO 2006

Will Shields ruled the line from his position at right guard. He was an excellent run blocker and even better at protecting the quarterback on passing plays. Shields made the Pro Bowl 12 years in a row.

TONY GONZALEZ   Tight End

- BORN: 2/27/1976   • PLAYED FOR TEAM: 1997 TO 2008

Tony Gonzalez starred in basketball and football in college. He chose to play for the Chiefs, and they were glad he did. Gonzalez was big, strong, and fast—and almost impossible to cover. He led the NFL with 102 catches in 2004.

PRIEST HOLMES   Running Back

- BORN: 10/7/1973

- PLAYED FOR TEAM: 2001 TO 2007

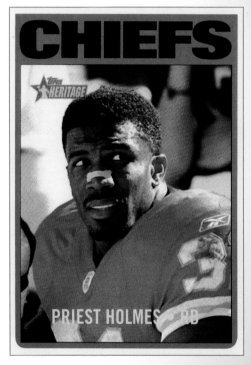

Priest Holmes proved that big things come in small packages. Though he stood just 5′ 9″, he was a swift and powerful runner. Holmes led the NFL in rushing yards in 2001 and in rushing touchdowns in 2002 and 2003.

DWAYNE BOWE   Receiver

- BORN: 9/21/1984

- FIRST YEAR WITH TEAM: 2007

In 2007, Dwayne Bowe led all NFL rookies with 70 receptions and six touchdown catches. He only got better from there. Bowe had more than 80 catches twice in his first five years with Kansas City and set a team record with 15 touchdowns in 2010.

LEFT: Will Shields
ABOVE: Priest Holmes

Calling the Shots

Starting a new sports league is risky business. That is why pro football owes so much to Lamar Hunt. When Hunt put the AFL together, he made sure its owners were smart and successful business leaders. He knew that the league would only be as strong as it weakest team. When the AFL became profitable, Hunt urged other owners to outbid the NFL for the best young players. The Chiefs made a big splash by signing Mike Garrett after he won the **Heisman Trophy** in 1965.

The AFL also needed coaches who could make the new league stand out to football fans. Hank Stram was the perfect man for the job. His most exciting players always got a chance to shine. Stram was also a good "salesman" for the AFL. He loved to talk football. Sometimes, he seemed more excited about his team than the fans were.

LEFT: Hank Stram and Lamar Hunt
RIGHT: Herman Edwards

Stram coached the Chiefs from 1960 to 1974. During that time, he won 124 games and four championships, three in the AFL and one in the NFL. Stram set a high standard for every coach that followed him.

The Chiefs found more remarkable football minds to lead the team. Marv Levy, Marty Schottenheimer, Dick Vermeil, and Herman Edwards all ranked among the most respected coaches of their time. Schottenheimer won more than 100 games with the Chiefs and led them to the 1993 AFC Championship Game. Under Vermeil, the team had the NFL's top-ranked offense three years in a row.

Although it has been a long time since the Chiefs have won a Super Bowl, the head job in Kansas City is one that attracts the top coaches whenever it is available. In 2011, the team hired Romeo Crennel. Crennel's first win as a Chief came against the unbeaten Green Bay Packers.

One Great Day

Before Super Bowl IV, just about everyone expected the Minnesota Vikings to win their first championship. The Vikings had a great defense that allowed very few points. Their offense could also be overpowering. Minnesota was favored to beat the Chiefs by two touchdowns.

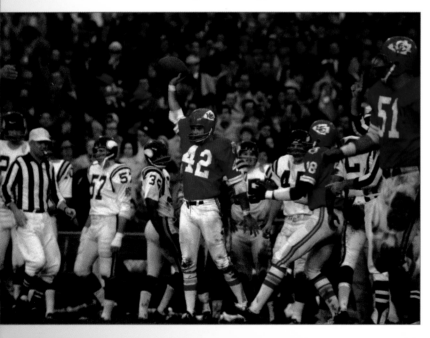

As kickoff neared, Kansas City coach Hank Stram and his players had heard enough about the Vikings. The Chiefs were eager to prove that they were the better team. The Vikings quickly learned that they were in for a long day. Buck Buchanan and Curley Culp clogged up the middle of

LEFT: Johnny Robinson celebrates his interception against the Minnesota Vikings.
RIGHT: This card of Otis Taylor came out a few months after Super Bowl IV.

OTIS TAYLOR
CHIEFS
WIDE RECEIVER

the **line of scrimmage**, and Bobby Bell, Willie Lanier, and Jim Lynch made tackles all over the field. Johnny Robinson led the charge against Minnesota's passing game.

The offense, meanwhile, was able to move the ball into range for Jan Stenerud to kick three field goals. With Kansas City leading 9–0, the Vikings fumbled, and the Chiefs recovered deep in Minnesota territory. Moments later, Mike Garrett scored a touchdown to increase the lead.

The Vikings fought back in the third quarter, but Len Dawson put an end to the comeback. He guided the Chiefs right back down the field. The key play was a short pass to Otis Taylor, who broke two tackles and ran 41 yards for a thrilling touchdown. Kansas City shut down the Vikings in the fourth quarter. Lanier, Robinson, and Emmitt Thomas each intercepted a pass. The final score was 23–7. The Chiefs were world champions!

Legend Has It

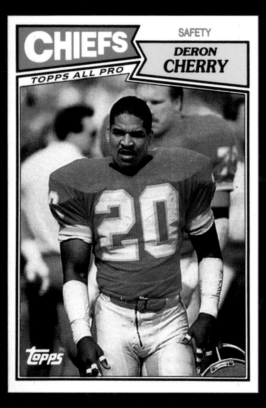

Did the Chiefs cut one of their greatest players in 1981?

LEGEND HAS IT that they did. Deron Cherry got a tryout as a punter with the Chiefs in the summer of 1981. He lost the job to Bob Grupp, and Kansas City sent him packing. About a month later, Cherry's phone rang. The Chiefs wanted him back. They knew he had also played safety in college and needed him to join their defense. Cherry became a star and stayed with the team for 11 seasons.

ABOVE: As this trading card shows, Deron Cherry became an All-Pro safety for the Chiefs.

Did a Chief once get tackled by the goal post?

LEGEND HAS IT that one did. During the 1960s, the goal post was located just inside the end zone. Once in a game, Len Dawson handed off to Jerrel Wilson deep in Kansas City territory. Wilson looked for a hole to run through but somehow didn't see the goal post. He ran right into it and fell in his own end zone for a **safety**. The Chiefs found another use for Wilson. They turned him into a punter, and soon he became the AFL's best. Dawson once said Wilson kicked the ball so hard he thought it might explode.

Was the Super Bowl named after a little girl's toy?

LEGEND HAS IT that it was. When the NFL and AFL were planning to become one league, the owners got tired of saying "NFL-AFL Championship Game." One day, Lamar Hunt called the game the Super Bowl. "I don't know where the term came from," Hunt said, "except that my daughter Sharon had a Super Ball—a little rubber ball with amazing bouncing ability ... So it must have come from that."

When the Chiefs traded for Matt Cassel in 2009, the fans in Kansas City weren't entirely sure what kind of quarterback they were getting. For three years, Cassel had been the backup to Tom Brady for the New England Patriots. When Brady was lost for the 2008 season with an injury, Cassel got his chance to start. He made the most of the opportunity. In 15 games, he threw for 3,693 yards and 21 touchdowns.

But before that, Cassel was a mystery man. In college, at the University of Southern California, he had not started a single game. In fact, he had

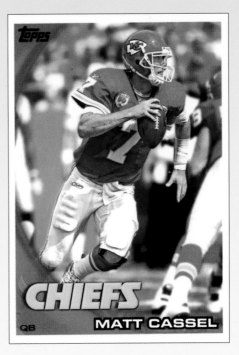

only thrown 33 passes in four years. After joining the Patriots, Cassel sat on the bench for three more seasons.

The Chiefs needed a new quarterback, and they were willing to take a chance. But as luck would have it, Cassel injured his knee in a **preseason** game—right after he signed a big contract! He limped through the entire season, and Kansas City went 4–12. The fans were grumbling that the Chiefs made a bad deal.

In 2010, those same fans couldn't have been happier. Cassel had a great year. Even emergency surgery in December did not slow him down. Cassel recovered from the operation and guided the Chiefs to *clutch* victories in the season's final two weeks. The Chiefs were AFC West champions for the first time in seven seasons.

The experts started leafing through the record books and made a surprising discovery. Cassel had made history. No quarterback had ever led his team to the playoffs without ever starting a college game.

There are few places more fun to watch a football game than Arrowhead Stadium. Fans arrive in the parking lot several hours before kickoff to meet with friends and have tailgate parties. The barbecue meals they serve are legendary. During the games, fans sing songs and shout special chants.

For their first 25 years in Kansas City, the Chiefs had a beautiful horse named Warpaint as their *mascot*. In 1989, a new mascot took over. K.C. Wolf was named after the "Wolfpack," one of the team's most famous group of fans.

Another favorite of the fans is the TD Pack Band. They set up behind the end zone and play music during the game. Tony "Mr. Music" DiPardo started the band. His daughter, Patti, took over many years ago. Mr. Music was still playing his trumpet in the band in his 90s!

LEFT: Fans celebrate with Bernard Pollard after a big play. He spent three seasons in a Kansas City uniform.   **ABOVE**: Fans bought this pin at home games during the 1960s.

n this timeline, each Super Bowl is listed under the year it was played. Remember that the Super Bowl is held early in the year and is actually part of the previous season. For example, Super Bowl XLVI was played on February 5, 2012, but it was the championship of the 2011 NFL season.

1974
Emmitt Thomas leads the NFL with 12 interceptions.

1962
The Texans win the AFL championship.

1960
The team plays its first season as the Dallas Texans.

1963
The Chiefs play their first season in Kansas City.

1970
The Chiefs win Super Bowl IV.

Bobby Bell was a star for the Kansas City teams of the 1960s.

Bobby
BELL
K. C. CHIEFS · LINEBACKER

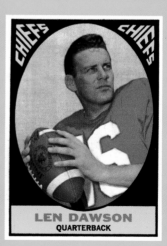

Len Dawson led the Chiefs to victory in Super Bowl IV.

LEN DAWSON
QUARTERBACK

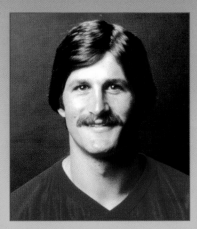

Bill
Kenney

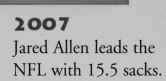

Dante
Hall

1983
Bill Kenney leads the AFC with 4,348 passing yards.

2002
Dante Hall scores on a punt and kickoff return in the same game.

2007
Jared Allen leads the NFL with 15.5 sacks.

1989
Christian Okoye leads the NFL in rushing.

1993
Joe Montana leads the Chiefs to the AFC Championship Game.

2010
Jamaal Charles is named All-Pro.

Christian
Okoye

Fun Facts

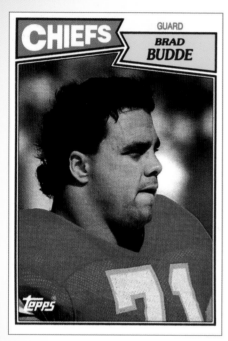

BUDDE SYSTEM

From 1963 to 1986, the Chiefs had a "Budde" playing left guard in all but three seasons. Ed Budde was the heart of the team's offensive line in the 1960s and 1970s. His son Brad starred for the Chiefs in the 1980s.

OH, SISTER!

Art Still led the Chiefs in sacks six times during the 1970s and 1980s. His sister, Valerie, was a basketball star for the University of Kentucky. She holds the school's record for career points by a male or female player.

36

ABOVE: Can you see the resemblance between Brad Budde (top) and his father (bottom)?   **RIGHT**: It's good! Nick Lowery celebrates another field goal.

MR. ACCURATE

Nick Lowery was the NFL's most accurate kicker during his 14 seasons with the Chiefs. He made the highest percentage of field goals in the league three times.

LIFE SAVER

In 1981, Joe Delaney set a Chiefs record with 1,121 rushing yards. During the summer two years later, Delaney saw three little boys drowning in a pond. He did not know how to swim but dove in anyway. Delaney was able to save one of the boys before he himself drowned.

TOUCHDOWN MAKER

In 2002, Priest Holmes broke Abner Haynes's team mark for touchdowns in a season with 21. The record had stood for 40 years. Holmes topped that mark a year later with 27 touchdowns.

GO, GARY, GO!

In a 1977 game against the Seattle Seahawks, Gary Barbaro intercepted a pass in the end zone. He ran it back 102 yards for a touchdown, which tied an NFL record at the time.

Talking Football

"You cannot win if you cannot run."
> **Hank Stram,** *on the importance of a good rushing attack*

"He was an innovator. He wasn't afraid to try new things."
> **Lamar Hunt,** *on Hank Stram, who was voted into the Hall of Fame in 2003*

"I don't ever recall any game I ever played that I didn't think we were going to win."
> **Len Dawson,** *on the confidence of the Chiefs in the 1960s and 1970s*

"I love this city. It's been my family."
> **Deron Cherry,** *on his fans and friends in Kansas City*

ABOVE: Hank Stram   **RIGHT:** Dwayne Bowe

"They want to double me? They can double me!"

► **Dwayne Bowe,** *on the challenge of being double-teamed on pass plays*

"He changed the tight end position. He's one of the best that's ever been around."

► **Otis Taylor,** *on Tony Gonzalez*

"You can't win a championship with just one or two people. It has to be the whole team."

► **Bobby Bell,** *on the key to the team's success in the 1960s*

"You can't let the pain get to you or you can't play this game … injuries just happen and you can't do anything about it."

► **Neil Smith,** *on playing your best with aches and pains*

"Nobody can predict the future, but I truly believe we can have a lot of success here."

► **Matt Cassel,** *on Kansas City's chances of returning to the Super Bowl*

Great Debates

People who root for the Chiefs love to compare their favorite moments, teams, and players. Some debates have been going on for years! How would you settle these classic football arguments?

Buck Buchanan was the Chiefs' greatest pass-rusher ...

... because opponents had to use two blockers on him on every play. If they didn't, Buchanan would plow right up the middle to get the quarterback. He was very tall and fast. If Buchanan had not been a football star, he probably could have played pro basketball. He made the Pro Bowl every year from 1964 to 1971.

The numbers tell a different story. Derrick Thomas was Kansas City's "chief" sack-master ...

... because his pass-rushing helped the Chiefs win more games than any team during the 1990s. Oh, and there was another number. Thomas (LEFT) led the NFL with 20 sacks in just his second season. He had seven sacks in one game that year! He ended his career with 126.5 sacks. Thomas was so dangerous that he changed the way opponents played the Chiefs.

The Kansas City teams of the 1990s would beat the Kansas City teams of the 1960s ....

… because they were faster and more explosive. The team's offense could score in many different ways. Marcus Allen led the running attack, and Willie Davis was a speedy receiver. Kansas City's quarterback was Joe Montana (RIGHT), one of the greatest passers ever. The Chiefs also had a **dominant** defense. Derrick Thomas, Neil Smith, James Hasty, and Dale Carter all had the ability to make game-changing plays.

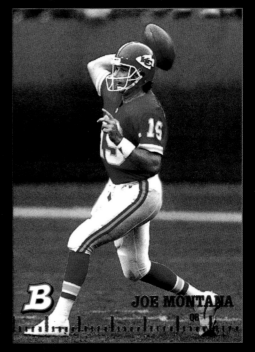

JOE MONTANA

The Chiefs of the 1960s would win easily ....

… because they were tougher and more talented at almost every position. Teams hated to play the Chiefs in the 1960s. They won an AFL title in Dallas in 1962 and two more in Kansas City in 1966 and 1969. Anyone who saw the Chiefs destroy the Minnesota Vikings in Super Bowl IV knew they were one of the best all-around teams in history.

For the Record

T he great Chiefs teams and players have left their marks on the record books. These are the "best of the best" …

Bill Maas

Priest Holmes

CHIEFS AWARD WINNERS

WINNER	AWARD	YEAR
Abner Haynes	AFL Most Valuable Player	1960
Abner Haynes	AFL Rookie of the Year	1960
Curtis McClinton	AFL Rookie of the Year	1962
Hank Stram	AFL Coach of the Year	1968
Len Dawson	Super Bowl IV MVP	1969
Bill Maas	NFL Defensive Rookie of the Year	1984
Derrick Thomas	NFL Defensive Rookie of the Year	1989
Barry Word	NFL Comeback Player of the Year	1990
Dale Carter	NFL Defensive Rookie of the Year	1992
Marcus Allen	NFL Comeback Player of the Year	1993
Priest Holmes	NFL Offensive Player of the Year	2002

51 JIM LYNCH 1967-77

Jim Lynch, a star for the 1969 champs, is one of many former players honored by the Chiefs.

CHIEFS ACHIEVEMENTS

ACHIEVEMENT	YEAR
AFL West Champions	1962
AFL Champions	1962
AFL West Champions	1966
AFL Champions	1966
AFL Champions	1969
Super Bowl IV Champions	1969*
AFC West Champions	1971
AFC West Champions	1993
AFC West Champions	1995
AFC West Champions	1997
AFC West Champions	2003
AFC West Champions	2010

Super Bowls are played early the following year, but the game is counted as the championship of this season.

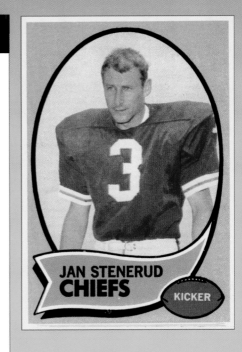

JAN STENERUD
CHIEFS
KICKER

ABOVE: Jan Stenerud was the kicker for the 1969 Super Bowl champs.
LEFT: Donnie Edwards was a defensive star for Kansas City in the 1990s.

Pinpoints

he history of a football team is made up of many smaller stories. These stories take place all over the map—not just in the city a team calls "home." Match the pushpins on these maps to the **Team Facts**, and you will begin to see the story of the Chiefs unfold!

TEAM FACTS

1 Kansas City, Missouri—*The team has played here since 1963.*

2 Dallas, Texas—*The team played here as the Texans from 1960 to 1962.*

3 Torrance, California—*Tony Gonzalez was born here.*

4 St. Louis, Missouri—*Trent Green was born here.*

5 Miami, Florida—*Derrick Thomas was born here.*

6 Shelby, North Carolina—*Bobby Bell was born here.*

7 Riverside, New Jersey—*Deron Cherry was born here.*

8 Buffalo, New York—*The Chiefs won the 1966 AFL championship here.*

9 Alliance, Ohio—*Len Dawson was born here.*

10 New Orleans, Louisiana—*The Chiefs won Super Bowl IV here.*

11 Fetsund, Norway—*Jan Stenerud was born here.*

12 Enugu, Nigeria—*Christian Okoye was born here.*

Tony Gonzalez

Glossary

🧠 Football Words
🧠 Vocabulary Words

AFC CHAMPIONSHIP GAME—The game played to determine which AFC team will go to the Super Bowl.

AFC WEST—A division for teams that play in the western part of the country.

AFL CHAMPIONSHIP GAME—The game that decided the winner of the AFL.

ALL-AFL—An honor given to the best players at each position in the AFL.

ALL-PRO—An honor given to the best players at their positions at the end of each season.

AMERICAN FOOTBALL CONFERENCE (AFC)—One of two groups of teams that make up the NFL.

AMERICAN FOOTBALL LEAGUE (AFL)—The football league that began play in 1960 and later merged with the NFL.

ARTIFICIAL TURF—A playing surface made from fake grass.

CLASSIC—Something that is popular for a long time.

CLUTCH—Timely and under pressure.

DOMINANT—Ruling or controlling.

ELUDED—Slipped away from.

FIELD GOAL—A goal from the field, kicked over the crossbar and between the goal posts. A field goal is worth three points.

HALL OF FAME—The museum in Canton, Ohio, where football's greatest players are honored.

HEISMAN TROPHY—The award given each year to the best player in college football.

INTERCEPTED—Caught in the air by a defensive player.

LINE OF SCRIMMAGE—The imaginary line that separates the offense and defense before each play begins.

MASCOT—An animal or person believed to bring a group good luck.

MOST VALUABLE PLAYER (MVP)—The award given each year to the league's best player; also given to the best player in the Super Bowl and Pro Bowl.

NATIONAL FOOTBALL LEAGUE (NFL)—The league that started in 1920 and is still operating today.

OVERTIME—The extra period played when a game is tied after 60 minutes.

PLAYOFFS—The games played after the regular season to determine which teams play in the Super Bowl.

POISE—Calm and confidence.

PRESEASON—Before the regular season.

PRO BOWL—The NFL's all-star game, played after the regular season.

PROFESSIONAL—Paid to play.

RIVALS—Extremely emotional competitors.

ROOKIE—A player in his first season.

SACK—Tackle the quarterback behind the line of scrimmage.

SAFETY—A tackle of a ball carrier in his own end zone. A safety is worth two points.

SUPER BOWL—The championship of the NFL, played between the winners of the National Football Conference and American Football Conference.

TRADEMARK—A special characteristic.

TRADITION—A belief or custom that is handed down from generation to generation.

WESTERN DIVISION—A group of teams that play in the western part of the country.

OVERTIME

TEAM SPIRIT introduces a great way to stay up to date with your team! Visit our **OVERTIME** link and get connected to the latest and greatest updates. **OVERTIME** serves as a young reader's ticket to an exclusive web page—with more stories, fun facts, team records, and photos of the Chiefs. Content is updated during and after each season. The **OVERTIME** feature also enables readers to send comments and letters to the author! Log onto:

www.norwoodhousepress.com/library.aspx

and click on the tab: **TEAM SPIRIT** to access **OVERTIME**.

Read all the books in the series to learn more about professional sports. For a complete listing of the baseball, basketball, football, and hockey teams in the **TEAM SPIRIT** series, visit our website at:

www.norwoodhousepress.com/library.aspx

On the Road

KANSAS CITY CHIEFS
One Arrowhead Drive
Kansas City, Missouri 64129
816–920-9300
www.kcchiefs.com

THE PRO FOOTBALL HALL OF FAME
2121 George Halas Drive NW
Canton, Ohio 44708
330-456-8207
www.profootballhof.com

On the Bookshelf

To learn more about the sport of football, look for these books at your library or bookstore:

- Frederick, Shane. *The Best of Everything Football Book.* North Mankato, Minnesota: Capstone Press, 2011.

- Jacobs, Greg. *The Everything Kids' Football Book: The All-Time Greats, Legendary Teams, Today's Superstars—And Tips on Playing Like a Pro.* Avon, Massachusetts: Adams Media Corporation, 2010.

- Editors of *Sports Illustrated for Kids. 1st and 10: Top 10 Lists of Everything in Football.* New York, New York: Sports Illustrated Books, 2011.

Index

PAGE NUMBERS IN **BOLD** REFER TO ILLUSTRATIONS.

About the Author

MARK STEWART has written more than 50 books on football and over 150 sports books for kids. He grew up in New York City during the 1960s rooting for the Giants and Jets, and was lucky enough to meet players from both teams. Mark comes from a family of writers. His grandfather was Sunday Editor of *The New York Times,* and his mother was Articles Editor of *Ladies' Home Journal* and *McCall's.* Mark has profiled hundreds of athletes over the past 25 years. He has also written several books about his native New York and New Jersey, his home today. Mark is a graduate of Duke University, with a degree in history. He lives and works in a home overlooking Sandy Hook, New Jersey. You can contact Mark through the Norwood House Press website.

ml

9-15